ANCIENT WISDOM IN HEBREW

48 Powerful Biblical Words on the Names and Truths of Scripture Every Christian Should Know

Theophilus Reed

Published by

GRAPEVINE BOOKS

www.grapevinebooks.com

email: grapevineindiapublishers@gmail.com

Ordering Information:

Quantity sales: Special discounts are available on quantity purchases by corporations, associations, and others.

For details, reach out to the publisher.

First published by Grapevine India Publishers Pvt Ltd 2025

CONTENTS

One

ELOHIM

אֱלֹהִים

God, the Creator

The Hebrew word **Elohim** is one of the most frequently used names for God in the Bible, appearing over 2,500 times. It is a plural form of **El**, meaning "God" or "Mighty One." Though plural in form, it is usually understood as singular in meaning when referring to the one true God, signifying majesty, power, and divine authority. The name **Elohim** is first used in **Genesis 1:1**, highlighting God's creative power.

Key Verses:

1. **Genesis 1:1** – *"In the beginning God (Elohim) created the heavens and the earth."*

2. **Deuteronomy 10:17** – *"For the Lord your God (YHWH Elohim) is God of gods and Lord of lords, the great God, mighty and awesome, who shows no partiality and accepts no bribes."*

3. **Psalm 19:1** – *"The heavens declare the glory of God (Elohim); the skies proclaim the work of his hands."*

4. **Isaiah 45:18** – *"For this is what the Lord says—He who created the heavens, He is God (Elohim); He who fashioned and made the earth, He founded it; He did not create it to be empty, but formed it to be*

inhabited—He says: 'I am the Lord, and there is no other.'"

5. **Psalm 46:1** – *"God (Elohim) is our refuge and strength, an ever-present help in trouble."*

The name **Elohim** emphasizes God's supreme power, sovereignty, and authority over all creation. Even though it is plural, it does not imply multiple gods but rather the fullness and greatness of God's being. Some Christian scholars also see the plural form as an early indication of the Trinity.

Two

YHWH

יְהוָה

The Sacred Name of God

YHWH (also written **Yahweh**) is the personal and most sacred name of God, revealed to Moses at the burning bush in **Exodus 3:14**, where God says, **"I Am Who I Am" (Ehyeh Asher Ehyeh).** The name **YHWH** is often translated as **LORD** in capital letters in English Bibles. It signifies God's eternal, self-existent nature—He is the same yesterday, today, and forever.

Key Verses:

1. **Exodus 3:14** – *"God said to Moses, 'I AM WHO I AM.' This is what you are to say to the Israelites: 'I AM has sent me to you.'"*
2. **Isaiah 42:8** – *"I am the LORD (YHWH); that is my name! I will not yield my glory to another or my praise to idols."*
3. **Psalm 83:18** – *"Let them know that you, whose name is the LORD (YHWH)—that you alone are the Most High over all the earth."*
4. **Jeremiah 10:10** – *"But the LORD (YHWH) is the true God; He is the living God, the eternal King."*
5. **Malachi 3:6** – *"I the LORD (YHWH) do not change. So you, the descendants of Jacob, are not destroyed."*

The name **YHWH** was considered so sacred that ancient Israelites avoided pronouncing it aloud, instead saying **Adonai (Lord)**. This name reflects God's unchanging and eternal nature, His faithfulness to His people, and His sovereignty over all creation. For Christians, Jesus' declaration **"Before Abraham was, I Am" (John 8:58)** is seen as an affirmation of His divinity, directly connecting Him to **YHWH**.

Three

Adonai

אֲדֹנָי

Lord, Master

The Hebrew word **Adonai** means "Lord" or "Master" and is used to express God's authority and sovereignty. While **YHWH** is God's sacred personal name, **Adonai** is often used as a respectful substitute, particularly in Jewish tradition. It signifies God's dominion over all creation and His rightful rule over His people.

Key Verses:

1. **Genesis 15:2** – *"But Abram said, 'Sovereign Lord (Adonai), what can you give me since I remain childless and the one who will inherit my estate is Eliezer of Damascus?'"*
2. **Exodus 4:10** – *"Moses said to the Lord (Adonai), 'Pardon your servant, Lord. I have never been eloquent, neither in the past nor since you have spoken to your servant. I am slow of speech and tongue.'"*
3. **Psalm 8:1** – *"Lord (Adonai), our Lord, how majestic is your name in all the earth! You have set your glory in the heavens."*
4. **Isaiah 6:1** – *"In the year that King Uzziah died, I saw the Lord (Adonai), high and exalted, seated on a throne; and the train of his robe filled the temple."*

5. **Daniel 9:19** – *"Lord (Adonai), listen! Lord, forgive! Lord, hear and act! For your sake, my God, do not delay, because your city and your people bear your Name."*

The word **Adonai** conveys reverence and submission, reminding believers that God is the supreme Master over their lives. Jesus is also referred to as **Adonai** in the New Testament, emphasizing His divine authority. When Paul writes, *"At the name of Jesus every knee should bow" (Philippians 2:10)*, it echoes the meaning of **Adonai**, signifying Jesus' lordship over all.

FOUR

EL SHADDAI

אֵל שַׁדַּי

GOD ALMIGHTY

El Shaddai is a powerful name of God that means **"God Almighty"** or **"The All-Sufficient One."** The exact meaning of **Shaddai** is debated, but it is often linked to divine strength and provision. **El Shaddai** emphasizes God's ability to sustain, bless, and protect His people.

Key Verses:

1. **Genesis 17:1** – *"When Abram was ninety-nine years old, the Lord appeared to him and said, 'I am God Almighty (El Shaddai); walk before me faithfully and be blameless.'"*

2. **Genesis 28:3** – *"May God Almighty (El Shaddai) bless you and make you fruitful and increase your numbers until you become a community of peoples."*

3. **Exodus 6:3** – *"I appeared to Abraham, to Isaac and to Jacob as God Almighty (El Shaddai), but by my name the Lord (YHWH) I did not make myself fully known to them."*

4. **Psalm 91:1** – *"Whoever dwells in the shelter of the Most High will rest in the shadow of the Almighty (Shaddai)."*

5. **Revelation 1:8** – *"'I am the Alpha and the Omega,' says the Lord God, 'who is, and who was, and who is to come, the Almighty (Pantokrator, equivalent to El Shaddai).'"*

The name **El Shaddai** reassures believers of God's might and sufficiency. In the Old Testament, it is often associated with God's blessings and covenant promises. For Christians, this name underscores God's ability to sustain His people in all circumstances, reminding them that He is both powerful and intimately involved in their lives.

Five

YHWH RAPHA

יְהוָה רָפָא

The Lord Who Heals

YHWH Rapha means **"The Lord Who Heals."** It highlights God's ability to restore physical, emotional, and spiritual health. This name appears in the Bible when God promises healing to the Israelites if they obey Him. It reassures believers that God is their healer, both in body and soul.

Key Verses:

1. **Exodus 15:26** – *"He said, 'If you listen carefully to the Lord your God (YHWH) and do what is right in His eyes, if you pay attention to His commands and keep all His decrees, I will not bring on you any of the diseases I brought on the Egyptians, for I am the Lord, who heals you (YHWH Rapha).'"*
2. **Psalm 103:2-3** – *"Praise the Lord, my soul, and forget not all His benefits—who forgives all your sins and heals all your diseases."*
3. **Jeremiah 17:14** – *"Heal me, Lord, and I will be healed; save me and I will be saved, for You are the one I praise."*
4. **Isaiah 53:5** – *"But He was pierced for our transgressions, He was crushed for our iniquities; the punishment that brought us peace was on Him, and by His wounds we are healed."*

5. **Matthew 8:16-17** – *"He drove out the spirits with a word and healed all the sick. This was to fulfill what was spoken through the prophet Isaiah: 'He took up our infirmities and bore our diseases.'"*

YHWH Rapha reminds believers that God cares for their well-being. While physical healing is part of this promise, the greatest healing comes through Jesus Christ, who restores people to God, heals their hearts, and grants eternal life.

Six

YHWH JIREH

יְהוָה יִרְאֶה

The Lord Who Provides

YHWH Jireh means **"The Lord Who Provides."** It comes from the story of Abraham and Isaac, where God provides a ram as a substitute sacrifice, showing His faithfulness in meeting His people's needs.

Key Verses:

1. **Genesis 22:14** – *"So Abraham called that place 'The Lord Will Provide (YHWH Jireh).' And to this day it is said, 'On the mountain of the Lord it will be provided.'"*
2. **Psalm 34:10** – *"The lions may grow weak and hungry, but those who seek the Lord lack no good thing."*
3. **Philippians 4:19** – *"And my God will meet all your needs according to the riches of His glory in Christ Jesus."*
4. **Matthew 6:31-33** – *"So do not worry, saying, 'What shall we eat?' or 'What shall we drink?' or 'What shall we wear?' But seek first His kingdom and His righteousness, and all these things will be given to you as well."*

SEVEN

YHWH NISSI

יְהוָה נִסִּי

THE LORD IS MY BANNER

YHWH Nissi means **"The Lord is My Banner."** This name was first revealed during Israel's battle against the Amalekites in **Exodus 17**. When Moses raised his hands, Israel prevailed; when he lowered them, Amalek gained ground. With God's help, Israel won, and Moses built an altar, declaring that the Lord was their **banner**, a symbol of victory and divine protection.

Key Verses:

1. **Exodus 17:15** – *"Moses built an altar and called it 'The Lord is my Banner (YHWH Nissi).'"*
2. **Psalm 60:4** – *"But for those who fear you, you have raised a banner to be unfurled against the bow."*
3. **Isaiah 11:10** – *"In that day the Root of Jesse will stand as a banner for the peoples; the nations will rally to him, and his resting place will be glorious."*
4. **Song of Solomon 2:4** – *"Let him lead me to the banquet hall, and let his banner over me be love."*
5. **1 Corinthians 15:57** – *"But thanks be to God! He gives us the victory*

through our Lord Jesus Christ."

YHWH Nissi signifies God's presence in battles—both physical and spiritual. In the New Testament, Jesus is seen as the ultimate **banner**, lifted up to bring salvation to the world. Just as banners were raised in battle for direction and encouragement, believers look to Christ for guidance and victory in life's struggles.

EIGHT

YHWH SHALOM

יְהוָה שָׁלוֹם

THE LORD IS PEACE

YHWH Shalom means **"The Lord Is Peace."** This name was first revealed to **Gideon** when God called him to deliver Israel from the Midianites. Though Gideon was afraid, God reassured him of His peace, leading Gideon to build an altar named **YHWH Shalom**.

Key Verses:

1. **Judges 6:24** – *"So Gideon built an altar to the Lord there and called it 'The Lord is Peace (YHWH Shalom).'"*

2. **Numbers 6:24-26** – *"The Lord bless you and keep you; the Lord make His face shine on you and be gracious to you; the Lord turn His face toward you and give you peace."*

3. **Isaiah 26:3** – *"You will keep in perfect peace those whose minds are steadfast, because they trust in you."*

4. **John 14:27** – *"Peace I leave with you; my peace I give you. I do not give to you as the world gives. Do not let your hearts be troubled and do not be afraid."*

5. **Philippians 4:7** – *"And the peace of God, which transcends all*

understanding, will guard your hearts and your minds in Christ Jesus."

YHWH Shalom assures believers that God's peace is not just the absence of conflict but a deep, spiritual well-being found in His presence. Jesus, called the **Prince of Peace (Isaiah 9:6),** fulfills this name by reconciling humanity with God through His sacrifice.

NINE

YHWH TSIDKENU

יְהוָה צִדְקֵנוּ

THE LORD OUR RIGHTEOUSNESS

YHWH Tsidkenu means **"The Lord Our Righteousness."** This name is introduced by the prophet **Jeremiah**, who foretells the coming of a righteous King from David's line. It emphasizes that righteousness does not come from human effort but is a gift from God. In the New Testament, Jesus Christ fulfills this name, as He is the **source of righteousness** for all who believe in Him.

Key Verses:

1. **Jeremiah 23:6** – *"In his days Judah will be saved and Israel will live in safety. This is the name by which he will be called: The Lord Our Righteousness (YHWH Tsidkenu)."*

2. **Jeremiah 33:16** – *"In those days Judah will be saved, and Jerusalem will live in safety. This is the name by which it will be called: The Lord Our Righteousness."*

3. **Isaiah 61:10** – *"I delight greatly in the Lord; my soul rejoices in my God. For He has clothed me with garments of salvation and arrayed me in a robe of His righteousness."*

4. **2 Corinthians 5:21** – *"God made Him who had no sin to be sin for us, so that in Him we might become the righteousness of God."*

5. **Romans 3:22** – *"This righteousness is given through faith in Jesus Christ to all who believe."*

YHWH Tsidkenu assures believers that righteousness is found in God alone. Jesus, as the **Messiah**, became righteousness for His followers, offering them a way to stand justified before God. This name reminds Christians that salvation is a gift, not something earned, and calls them to live righteously through faith in Christ.

TEN

YHWH SABAOTH

יְהוָה צְבָאוֹת

THE LORD OF HOSTS

YHWH Sabaoth means **"The Lord of Hosts"** or **"The Lord of Armies."** This name emphasizes God's supreme command over heavenly and earthly forces. It appears often in the prophetic books, especially in times of war and spiritual conflict. It highlights God's might, authority, and ability to protect His people.

Key Verses:

1. **1 Samuel 17:45** – *"David said to the Philistine, 'You come against me with sword and spear and javelin, but I come against you in the name of the Lord of Hosts (YHWH Sabaoth), the God of the armies of Israel, whom you have defied.'"*

2. **Psalm 24:10** – *"Who is He, this King of glory? The Lord of Hosts (YHWH Sabaoth)—He is the King of glory."*

3. **Isaiah 6:3** – *"And they were calling to one another: 'Holy, holy, holy is the Lord of Hosts (YHWH Sabaoth); the whole earth is full of His glory.'"*

4. **Jeremiah 10:16** – *"The Portion of Jacob is not like these, for He is the Maker of all things, including Israel, the tribe of His inheritance—the Lord of Hosts is His name."*

5. **James 5:4** – *"Look! The wages you failed to pay the workers who mowed your fields are crying out against you. The cries of the harvesters have reached the ears of the Lord of Hosts (Kyrios Sabaoth)."*

YHWH Sabaoth reveals God as the **Commander of angelic armies**, ensuring victory for His people. In the New Testament, Jesus is portrayed as leading the heavenly hosts in the final battle against evil (**Revelation 19:11-14**). This name reassures believers that they are not alone in spiritual warfare—God fights for them, and His power is greater than any force against them.

ELEVEN

MASHIACH

מָשִׁיחַ

MESSIAH, THE ANOINTED ONE

The Hebrew word **Mashiach** means **"Messiah"** or **"Anointed One."** In the Old Testament, anointing with oil was a sign of being set apart for God's purpose—whether as a king, priest, or prophet. The Jewish people awaited the **Mashiach**, a divinely appointed ruler who would establish God's kingdom. In the New Testament, Jesus is recognized as the **Messiah**, fulfilling prophecies of the **Anointed One** who would bring salvation.

Key Verses:

1. **Daniel 9:25-26** – *"Know and understand this: From the time the word goes out to restore and rebuild Jerusalem until the Anointed One (Mashiach), the ruler, comes, there will be seven 'sevens,' and sixty-two 'sevens.'"*

2. **Isaiah 61:1** – *"The Spirit of the Lord is on me, because the Lord has anointed me to proclaim good news to the poor."* (Jesus quotes this in **Luke 4:18**.)

3. **Psalm 2:2** – *"The kings of the earth rise up and the rulers band together against the Lord and against His Anointed (Mashiach)."*

4. **John 1:41** – *"The first thing Andrew did was to find his brother Simon*

and tell him, 'We have found the Messiah' (that is, the Christ)."

5. **Matthew 16:16** – *"Simon Peter answered, 'You are the Messiah, the Son of the living God.'"*

Mashiach is central to Christian belief. The New Testament refers to Jesus as **Christos**, the Greek equivalent of **Mashiach**. Jesus fulfilled Old Testament prophecies, showing that He is not only the anointed King but also the suffering servant who redeems humanity.

TWELVE

YESHUA

יֵשׁוּעַ

JESUS

Yeshua is the Hebrew name for **Jesus**, meaning **"Salvation" or "The Lord Saves."** It is derived from **Yehoshua**, the full name of **Joshua**. The name emphasizes Jesus' role as the Savior of the world. When the angel told Mary and Joseph to name their son **Yeshua**, it was because He would **save His people from their sins (Matthew 1:21).**

Key Verses:

1. **Matthew 1:21** – *"She will give birth to a son, and you are to give Him the name Jesus (Yeshua), because He will save His people from their sins."*
2. **Luke 2:30-32** – *"For my eyes have seen your salvation (Yeshua), which you have prepared in the sight of all nations."*
3. **Acts 4:12** – *"Salvation is found in no one else, for there is no other name under heaven given to mankind by which we must be saved."*
4. **John 14:6** – *"Jesus answered, 'I am the way and the truth and the life. No one comes to the Father except through me.'"*
5. **Philippians 2:9-10** – *"God exalted Him to the highest place and gave Him the name that is above every name, that at the name of Jesus*

> *(Yeshua) every knee should bow, in heaven and on earth and under the earth."*

The name **Yeshua** reflects Jesus' mission to bring salvation to all. In Hebrew thought, names carry deep significance, and **Yeshua's name itself proclaims the gospel—God's desire to save humanity.** Many Messianic Jews refer to Jesus as **Yeshua HaMashiach (Jesus the Messiah),** emphasizing His fulfillment of biblical prophecy.

THIRTEEN

TORAH

תּוֹרָה

THE LAW, INSTRUCTION

The Hebrew word **Torah** means **"law," "instruction," or "teaching."** It primarily refers to the first five books of the Bible (**Genesis, Exodus, Leviticus, Numbers, and Deuteronomy**), also called the **Pentateuch**. The Torah contains God's commandments, guiding His people in how to live a holy and righteous life. In Christianity, Jesus is seen as the fulfillment of the Torah, bringing its deeper spiritual meaning to light.

Key Verses:

1. **Joshua 1:8** – *"Keep this Book of the Law (Torah) always on your lips; meditate on it day and night, so that you may be careful to do everything written in it. Then you will be prosperous and successful."*

2. **Psalm 1:2** – *"But whose delight is in the law of the Lord (Torah), and who meditates on His law day and night."*

3. **Psalm 119:105** – *"Your word is a lamp for my feet, a light on my path."*

4. **Matthew 5:17** – *"Do not think that I have come to abolish the Law (Torah) or the Prophets; I have not come to abolish them but to fulfill them."*

5. **Romans 3:31** – *"Do we, then, nullify the law by this faith? Not at all! Rather, we uphold the law."*

For Christians, the Torah serves as a **moral foundation** that points toward Christ. Jesus did not abolish it but fulfilled its deeper spiritual meaning, making righteousness accessible through faith rather than legalistic observance.

FOURTEEN

B'RIT HADASHAH

בְּרִית חֲדָשָׁה

NEW COVENANT

B'rit Hadashah means **"New Covenant."** In the Old Testament, God made covenants with **Noah, Abraham, Moses, and David**. The **New Covenant** was prophesied by **Jeremiah**, and Jesus established it at the Last Supper, fulfilling God's promise to bring salvation to all people through faith in Him.

Key Verses:

1. **Jeremiah 31:31** *"'The days are coming,' declares the Lord, 'when I will make a new covenant (B'rit Hadashah) with the people of Israel and with the people of Judah.'"*

2. **Ezekiel 36:26-27** – *"I will give you a new heart and put a new spirit in you; I will remove from you your heart of stone and give you a heart of flesh. And I will put my Spirit in you and move you to follow my decrees and be careful to keep my laws."*

3. **Luke 22:20** – *"In the same way, after the supper He took the cup, saying, 'This cup is the new covenant (B'rit Hadashah) in my blood, which is poured out for you.'"*

4. **Hebrews 8:6** – *"But in fact, the ministry Jesus has received is as superior to theirs as the covenant of which He is mediator is superior to the old one,*

since the new covenant is established on better promises."

5. **2 Corinthians 3:6** – *"He has made us competent as ministers of a new covenant—not of the letter but of the Spirit; for the letter kills, but the Spirit gives life."*

The **B'rit Hadashah** is the **covenant of grace**, replacing the old sacrificial system with **Jesus' atoning sacrifice.** Under this covenant, righteousness is obtained **through faith, not works**, and believers receive the **Holy Spirit** to guide them in truth.

FIFTEEN

NEVI'IM

נְבִיאִים

PROPHETS

The Hebrew word **Nevi'im** means **"Prophets"** and refers to the second section of the **Tanakh (Hebrew Bible)**. It includes books written by prophets such as **Isaiah, Jeremiah, Ezekiel, and the twelve minor prophets.** These books contain prophecies about Israel, warnings of judgment, and promises of restoration. Many of these prophecies point to the **coming of the Messiah, Jesus Christ.**

Key Verses:

1. **Deuteronomy 18:18** – *"I will raise up for them a prophet like you from among their fellow Israelites, and I will put My words in his mouth. He will tell them everything I command him."*
2. **Isaiah 7:14** – *"Therefore the Lord Himself will give you a sign: The virgin will conceive and give birth to a son, and will call Him Immanuel."*
3. **Jeremiah 1:5** – *"Before I formed you in the womb I knew you, before you were born I set you apart; I appointed you as a prophet to the nations."*
4. **Matthew 5:17** – *"Do not think that I have come to abolish the Law or the Prophets (Nevi'im); I have not come to abolish them but to fulfill*

them."

5. **Acts 3:22** – *"For Moses said, 'The Lord your God will raise up for you a prophet like me from among your own people; you must listen to everything He tells you.'"*

The **Nevi'im** confirm God's sovereignty, justice, and mercy. Jesus is recognized as the ultimate fulfillment of prophetic writings, as He embodies the promised **Messiah and Redeemer.**

SIXTEEN

KETUVIM

כְּתוּבִים

WRITINGS

The Hebrew word **Ketuvim** means **"Writings"** and is the third section of the **Tanakh (Hebrew Bible)**. It includes books like **Psalms, Proverbs, Job, Ecclesiastes, Song of Songs, and historical books like Ruth and Esther.** These writings offer wisdom, poetry, and reflections on faith and human ex perience.

Key Verses:

1. **Psalm 19:7** – *"The law of the Lord is perfect, refreshing the soul. The statutes of the Lord are trustworthy, making wise the simple."*
2. **Proverbs 3:5-6** – *"Trust in the Lord with all your heart and lean not on your own understanding; in all your ways submit to Him, and He will make your paths straight."*
3. **Ecclesiastes 12:13** – *"Now all has been heard; here is the conclusion of the matter: Fear God and keep His commandments, for this is the duty of all mankind."*
4. **Luke 24:44** – *"He said to them, 'This is what I told you while I was still with you: Everything must be fulfilled that is written about Me in the Law of Moses, the Prophets, and the Psalms (Ketuvim).'"*

5. **2 Timothy 3:16** – *"All Scripture is God-breathed and is useful for teaching, rebuking, correcting and training in righteousness."*

The **Ketuvim** provide wisdom and encouragement for believers. Jesus referenced these writings to confirm that His life and mission fulfilled **God's plan as recorded in Scripture.** Through Psalms and Proverbs, Christians gain insight into **worship, faith, and righteous living.**

Seventeen

SHABBAT

שַׁבָּת

Sabbath, The Day of Rest

The Hebrew word **Shabbat** means **"Sabbath" or "rest."** It originates from **Genesis 2:2-3**, where God rested on the seventh day after creation. In Jewish tradition, Shabbat is observed from **Friday evening to Saturday evening**, serving as a day of worship and rest. For Christians, **Jesus fulfills the Sabbath** by offering spiritual rest through salvation.

Key Verses:

1. **Genesis 2:2-3** – *"By the seventh day God had finished the work He had been doing; so on the seventh day He rested from all His work. Then God blessed the seventh day and made it holy."*
2. **Exodus 20:8-10** – *"Remember the Sabbath day by keeping it holy. Six days you shall labor and do all your work, but the seventh day is a Sabbath to the Lord your God."*
3. **Isaiah 58:13-14** – *"If you call the Sabbath a delight and the Lord's holy day honorable... then you will find your joy in the Lord."*
4. **Mark 2:27-28** – *"Then He said to them, 'The Sabbath was made for man, not man for the Sabbath. So the Son of Man is Lord even of the Sabbath.'"*

5. **Hebrews 4:9-10** – *"There remains, then, a Sabbath-rest for the people of God; for anyone who enters God's rest also rests from their works, just as God did from His."*

Shabbat reminds believers of **God's provision and rest.** While the Jewish people observe it as a weekly day of rest, **Jesus offers eternal rest**, making every day an opportunity to abide in Him.

EIGHTEEN

PESACH

פֶּסַח

PASSOVER

Pesach, or **Passover**, is a major Jewish festival commemorating Israel's **deliverance from slavery in Egypt.** It originates from the final plague, where the **blood of a lamb** marked the Israelites' doors, sparing them from death (**Exodus 12**). Christians see **Jesus as the ultimate Passover Lamb**, whose blood grants salvation.

Key Verses:

1. **Exodus 12:13** – *"The blood will be a sign for you on the houses where you are, and when I see the blood, I will pass over you."*
2. **Leviticus 23:5** – *"The Lord's Passover begins at twilight on the fourteenth day of the first month."*
3. **Isaiah 53:7** – *"He was led like a lamb to the slaughter, and as a sheep before its shearers is silent, so He did not open His mouth."*
4. **John 1:29** – *"Look, the Lamb of God, who takes away the sin of the world!"*
5. **1 Corinthians 5:7** – *"For Christ, our Passover lamb, has been sacrificed."*

Pesach symbolizes **redemption and freedom.** Just as the Israelites were freed from physical slavery, **Jesus' sacrifice frees believers from sin and death, offering eternal life.** The Lord's Supper (**Communion**) reflects this, as Jesus connected His death to the **Passover meal (Luke 22:19-20).**

NINETEEN

HALLELUJAH

הַלְלוּיָהּ

PRAISE THE LORD

The Hebrew word **Hallelujah** is a combination of **"Hallel" meaning "praise,"** and **"Yah"**, a shortened form of **YHWH (the divine name of God).** It literally means **"Praise the Lord"** and is used frequently in the Psalms as an exclamation of worship and joy. In the New Testament, it is used in **Revelation**, where the heavenly hosts praise God's ultimate victory.

Key Verses:

1. **Psalm 146:1** – *"Praise the Lord (Hallelujah). Praise the Lord, my soul!"*
2. **Psalm 150:6** – *"Let everything that has breath praise the Lord (Hallelujah)!"*
3. **Revelation 19:1** – *"After this I heard what sounded like the roar of a great multitude in heaven shouting: 'Hallelujah! Salvation and glory and power belong to our God.'"*
4. **Revelation 19:6** – *"Then I heard what sounded like a great multitude, like the roar of rushing waters and like loud peals of thunder, shouting: 'Hallelujah! For our Lord God Almighty reigns!'"*
5. **Psalm 113:1** – *"Praise the Lord (Hallelujah)! Praise, O servants of the*

Lord, praise the name of the Lord."

Hallelujah is a universal word of praise, transcending languages and cultures. It reminds believers that God is worthy of worship, no matter the circumstances. In Christianity, **Jesus' victory over sin and death** is the greatest reason to say **Hallelujah!**

TWENTY

AMEN

אָמֵן

SO BE IT, TRUTH

The Hebrew word **Amen** means **"so be it" or "truth."** It signifies agreement, faithfulness, and affirmation. In Scripture, **Amen** is used to confirm prayers, blessings, and divine promises. Jesus often used **"Amen, amen" (Truly, truly)** to emphasize His teachings, showing **His authority as the Truth (John 14:6).**

Key Verses:

1. **Numbers 5:22** – *"Then the woman is to say, 'Amen. So be it.'"*
2. **Deuteronomy 27:26** – *"Cursed is anyone who does not uphold the words of this law by carrying them out. Then all the people shall say, 'Amen!'"*
3. **2 Corinthians 1:20** – *"For no matter how many promises God has made, they are 'Yes' in Christ. And so through Him the 'Amen' is spoken by us to the glory of God."*
4. **Revelation 3:14** – *"These are the words of the Amen, the faithful and true witness, the ruler of God's creation."*
5. **Revelation 22:20** – *"He who testifies to these things says, 'Yes, I am coming soon.' Amen. Come, Lord Jesus."*

Amen is more than just a closing word in prayers—it is a declaration of **trust in God's truth and faithfulness.** Jesus is called **"the Amen"**, meaning He is the **ultimate fulfillment of God's promises.**

TWENTY-ONE

TZEDAKAH

צְדָקָה

RIGHTEOUSNESS, CHARITY

The Hebrew word **Tzedakah** means **"righteousness"** but is often used to refer to **charity and justice.** In Jewish and biblical thought, giving to the poor is not just an act of kindness—it is a moral duty rooted in God's justice. In Christianity, Jesus taught that **true righteousness** comes from both **faith and love expressed through giving.**

Key Verses:

1. **Proverbs 21:3** – *"To do what is right and just (tzedakah) is more acceptable to the Lord than sacrifice."*
2. **Psalm 112:9** – *"They have freely scattered their gifts to the poor, their righteousness (tzedakah) endures forever."*
3. **Isaiah 1:17** – *"Learn to do right; seek justice. Defend the oppressed. Take up the cause of the fatherless; plead the case of the widow."*
4. **Matthew 6:1-2** – *"Be careful not to practice your righteousness (tzedakah) in front of others to be seen by them. When you give to the needy, do not announce it with trumpets."*
5. **2 Corinthians 9:9** – *"As it is written: 'They have freely scattered their*

gifts to the poor; their righteousness endures forever.'"

Tzedakah teaches that righteousness is not just about belief but about **action—helping those in need.** Jesus and the apostles emphasized that **true righteousness is demonstrated through love, generosity, and justice.**

TWENTY-TWO

MITZVAH

מִצְוָה

COMMANDMENT

The Hebrew word **Mitzvah** means **"commandment"** and refers to God's instructions in the Torah. There are **613 mitzvot (plural of mitzvah)** in Jewish tradition, including the **Ten Commandments.** In Christianity, Jesus summarized the commandments into **two great mitzvot: love God and love your neighbor.**

Key Verses:

1. **Deuteronomy 6:6** – *"These commandments (mitzvot) that I give you today are to be on your hearts."*
2. **Deuteronomy 11:1** – *"Love the Lord your God and keep His requirements, His decrees, His laws, and His commands (mitzvot) always."*
3. **Psalm 119:10-11** – *"I seek You with all my heart; do not let me stray from Your commands (mitzvot). I have hidden Your word in my heart that I might not sin against You."*
4. **Matthew 22:37-39** – *"Jesus replied: 'Love the Lord your God with all your heart and with all your soul and with all your mind.' This is the first and greatest commandment (mitzvah). And the second is like it:*

'Love your neighbor as yourself.'"

5. **John 14:15** – *"If you love me, keep my commandments (mitzvot)."*

Mitzvah reminds believers that obedience to God's will is not a burden but an **expression of love.** Jesus emphasized that **faith should be lived out** through obedience to God's greatest commandments—**loving God and loving others.**

Twenty-Three

TESHUVAH

תְּשׁוּבָה

Repentance, Returning to God

The Hebrew word **Teshuvah** means **"repentance"** or **"returning to God."** It comes from the root **shuv,** which means **"to turn back" or "to return."** In Jewish thought, teshuvah is not just feeling sorry for sin but a complete turning away from it and returning to God. In Christianity, repentance is essential for salvation, and Jesus preached **teshuvah** as part of His message of the Kingdom.

Key Verses:

1. **Ezekiel 18:30** – *"Repent (teshuvah) and turn from all your offenses; then sin will not be your downfall."*

2. **Joel 2:13** – *"Rend your heart and not your garments. Return (teshuvah) to the Lord your God, for He is gracious and compassionate, slow to anger and abounding in love."*

3. **Isaiah 55:7** – *"Let the wicked forsake their ways and the unrighteous their thoughts. Let them turn to the Lord, and He will have mercy on them."*

4. **Luke 5:32** – *"I have not come to call the righteous, but sinners to repentance (teshuvah)."*

5. **Acts 3:19** – *"Repent (teshuvah), then, and turn to God, so that your sins may be wiped out, that times of refreshing may come from the Lord."*

Teshuvah teaches that **God always welcomes those who turn back to Him.** Jesus fulfilled this concept by offering forgiveness and calling sinners to **turn from sin and follow Him.**

TWENTY-FOUR

SHALOM

שָׁלוֹם

PEACE, WHOLENESS

The Hebrew word **Shalom** means more than just **"peace"**—it refers to **completeness, wholeness, and well-being.** It signifies **spiritual, emotional, and physical peace** that comes from God. In the Bible, shalom is not just the absence of conflict but the **presence of God's blessings.** Jesus, as the **Prince of Peace (Sar Shalom),** brings ultimate shalom to the world.

Key Verses:

1. **Numbers 6:24-26** – *"The Lord bless you and keep you; the Lord make His face shine on you and be gracious to you; the Lord turn His face toward you and give you peace (shalom)."*
2. **Isaiah 26:3** – *"You will keep in perfect peace (shalom) those whose minds are steadfast, because they trust in You."*
3. **Psalm 29:11** – *"The Lord gives strength to His people; the Lord blesses His people with peace (shalom)."*
4. **John 14:27** – *"Peace (shalom) I leave with you; my peace I give you. I do not give to you as the world gives. Do not let your hearts be troubled and do not be afraid."*

5. **Philippians 4:7** – *"And the peace (shalom) of God, which transcends all understanding, will guard your hearts and your minds in Christ Jesus."*

Shalom is a gift from God, representing **fullness of life and harmony.** Jesus offers **true shalom, reconciling people with God** and bringing eternal peace through faith in Him.

TWENTY-FIVE

CHESED

חֶסֶד

LOVING-KINDNESS, MERCY

The Hebrew word **Chesed** is one of the most important words in the Bible, meaning **"loving-kindness," "mercy," "grace," or "steadfast love."** It describes **God's covenantal love**—His unwavering kindness and faithfulness toward His people. Chesed is more than just kindness; it is an enduring love that is both compassionate and committed.

Key Verses:

1. **Exodus 34:6** – *"The Lord, the Lord, the compassionate and gracious God, slow to anger, abounding in love (chesed) and faithfulness."*
2. **Psalm 136:26** – *"Give thanks to the God of heaven. His love (chesed) endures forever."*
3. **Micah 6:8** – *"He has shown you, O mortal, what is good. And what does the Lord require of you? To act justly and to love mercy (chesed) and to walk humbly with your God."*
4. **Lamentations 3:22-23** – *"Because of the Lord's great love (chesed) we are not consumed, for His compassions never fail. They are new every morning."*

5. **Titus 3:5** – *"He saved us, not because of righteous things we had done, but because of His mercy (chesed). He saved us through the washing of rebirth and renewal by the Holy Spirit."*

Chesed is central to both the Old and New Testaments. God's steadfast love is **unbreakable and unconditional**, culminating in **Jesus' sacrifice**, which demonstrates the highest form of chesed—God's mercy and grace toward sinners.

TWENTY-SIX

EMUNAH

אֱמוּנָה

FAITH, TRUST IN GOD

The Hebrew word **Emunah** means **"faith"** or **"trust."** It refers to **steadfastness, reliability, and complete dependence on God.** Unlike mere belief, emunah implies a **living faith—a deep confidence in God's promises and actions.** It is not just about knowing that God exists, but actively trusting Him in all circumstances.

Key Verses:

1. **Habakkuk 2:4** – *"The righteous shall live by his faith (emunah)."*
2. **Exodus 17:12** – *"When Moses' hands grew tired, they took a stone and put it under him, and he sat on it. Aaron and Hur held his hands up—one on one side, one on the other—so that his hands remained steady (emunah) till sunset."*
3. **Psalm 37:3** – *"Trust in the Lord and do good; dwell in the land and enjoy safe pasture."*
4. **Romans 1:17** – *"For in the gospel the righteousness of God is revealed—a righteousness that is by faith (emunah) from first to last, just as it is written: 'The righteous will live by faith.'"*

5. **Hebrews 11:1** – *"Now faith (emunah) is confidence in what we hope for and assurance about what we do not see."*

Emunah is more than intellectual belief—it is a **firm reliance on God, even when circumstances are uncertain.** In the New Testament, faith in **Jesus Christ** becomes the way to **salvation and righteousness**. True **emunah** leads to **obedience, perseverance, and trust** in God's unfailing plan.

Twenty-Seven

YIRAH

יִרְאָה

Fear of the Lord, Reverence

The Hebrew word **Yirah** means **"fear" or "awe,"** but in a biblical context, it often refers to **reverence and deep respect for God.** It is not a fear of terror but a recognition of **God's power, holiness, and authority.** The Bible teaches that **the fear of the Lord is the beginning of wisdom,** leading to a righteous life.

Key Verses:

1. **Proverbs 9:10** – *"The fear of the Lord (yirah) is the beginning of wisdom, and knowledge of the Holy One is understanding."*
2. **Psalm 111:10** – *"The fear of the Lord (yirah) is the beginning of wisdom; all who follow His precepts have good understanding."*
3. **Isaiah 33:6** – *"He will be the sure foundation for your times, a rich store of salvation and wisdom and knowledge; the fear of the Lord (yirah) is the key to this treasure."*
4. **Matthew 10:28** – *"Do not be afraid of those who kill the body but cannot kill the soul. Rather, be afraid (yirah) of the One who can destroy both soul and body in hell."*

5. **Philippians 2:12** – *"Work out your salvation with fear (yirah) and trembling."*

Yirah teaches that **a healthy fear of the Lord** leads to **wisdom, righteousness, and obedience.** Jesus reinforced this by teaching that true fear should be directed toward **God alone, not worldly fears.**

Twenty-Eight

TIKVAH

תִּקְוָה

Hope

The Hebrew word **Tikvah** means **"hope" or "expectation."** It is not just wishful thinking but **a confident assurance in God's promises.** Throughout the Bible, hope is linked to **God's faithfulness, salvation, and the coming of the Messiah.**

Key Verses:

1. **Jeremiah 29:11** – *"For I know the plans I have for you, declares the Lord, plans to prosper you and not to harm you, plans to give you hope (tikvah) and a future."*
2. **Psalm 71:5** – *"For You have been my hope (tikvah), Sovereign Lord, my confidence since my youth."*
3. **Lamentations 3:21-23** – *"Yet this I call to mind and therefore I have hope (tikvah): Because of the Lord's great love we are not consumed, for His compassions never fail."*
4. **Romans 15:13** – *"May the God of hope (tikvah) fill you with all joy and peace as you trust in Him, so that you may overflow with hope by the power of the Holy Spirit."*

5. **Hebrews 6:19** – *"We have this hope (tikvah) as an anchor for the soul, firm and secure."*

Tikvah reminds believers that **hope is rooted in God, not circumstances.** Jesus embodies **the ultimate hope**—eternal life and redemption through His resurrection.

TWENTY-NINE

MISHKAN

מִשְׁכָּן

TABERNACLE

Verses:

1. *Exodus 25:8* – "And let them make me a sanctuary, that I may dwell in their midst."
2. *Exodus 40:34* – "Then the cloud covered the Tent of Meeting, and the glory of the Lord filled the tabernacle."
3. *Leviticus 26:11* – "I will set my tabernacle among you, and my soul shall not abhor you."
4. *Numbers 9:15* – "On the day that the tabernacle was set up, the cloud covered the tabernacle, the tent of the testimony."
5. *2 Samuel 7:6* – "I have not lived in a house since the day I brought the Israelites up out of Egypt to this day, but I have moved from tent to tent, from one dwelling place to another."

Meaning: The *Mishkan* (Tabernacle) was a portable sanctuary built under divine instruction for Israel's worship in the wilderness. It was the dwelling place of God's presence, where sacrifices were offered and divine guidance was received. The Mishkan housed sacred objects such as the Ark of the Covenant and the Menorah, signifying holiness and devotion. It symbolized God's closeness to His people and was later replaced by the permanent structure of the Temple in Jerusalem.

THIRTY

BEIT HAMIKDASH

בֵּית הַמִּקְדָּשׁ

THE HOLY TEMPLE

Verses:

1. *1 Kings 6:1* – "In the four hundred and eightieth year after the Israelites came out of Egypt, in the fourth year of Solomon's reign over Israel, he began to build the temple of the Lord."

2. *2 Chronicles 7:16* – "I have chosen and consecrated this temple so that my Name may be there forever. My eyes and my heart will always be there."

3. *Isaiah 56:7* – "My house will be called a house of prayer for all nations."

4. *Psalm 122:1* – "I rejoiced with those who said to me, 'Let us go to the house of the Lord.'"

5. *Haggai 2:9* – "The glory of this present house will be greater than the glory of the former house, says the Lord Almighty. And in this place, I will grant peace."

Meaning: The *Beit HaMikdash* (Holy Temple) was the permanent dwelling of God's presence in Jerusalem. Built first by Solomon and later rebuilt after the Babylonian exile, it served as the center of worship, sacrifices, and national identity. The destruction of the First and Second Temples marked significant losses in Jewish history. Despite this, the hope for a future Third Temple remains a central element of Jewish eschatology, symbolizing redemption and divine restoration.

THIRTY-ONE

MENORAH

מְנוֹרָה

SEVEN-BRANCHED LAMPSTAND

Verses:

1. *Exodus 25:31* – "You shall make a lampstand of pure gold. The lampstand shall be made of hammered work; its base, its stem, its cups, its calyxes, and its flowers shall be of one piece with it."

2. *Exodus 27:20* – "Command the Israelites to bring you clear oil of pressed olives for the light so that the lamps may be kept burning."

3. *Zechariah 4:2* – "I see a solid gold lampstand with a bowl at the top and seven lamps on it, with seven channels to the lamps."

4. *Numbers 8:2* – "Speak to Aaron and say to him, 'When you set up the seven lamps, they are to light the area in front of the lampstand.'"

5. *Revelation 1:12* – "I turned around to see the voice that was speaking to me. And when I turned I saw seven golden lampstands."

Meaning: The *Menorah* is a seven-branched lampstand that was placed in the Tabernacle and later in the Temple, symbolizing divine wisdom and God's presence. It was to be continually lit with pure olive oil, representing spiritual enlightenment and the eternal flame of faith. The Menorah also signifies light overcoming darkness and is a powerful emblem of Judaism. The modern national emblem of Israel is inspired by the ancient Menorah.

THIRTY-TWO

KOHEN

כֹּהֵן

PRIEST

Verses:

1. *Exodus 28:1* – "Have Aaron your brother brought to you from among the Israelites, along with his sons Nadab, Abihu, Eleazar, and Ithamar, so they may serve me as priests."

2. *Leviticus 21:6* – "They shall be holy to their God and not profane the name of their God, for they offer the Lord's food offerings, the bread of their God; therefore they shall be holy."

3. *Numbers 18:7* – "But only you and your sons may serve as priests in connection with everything at the altar and inside the curtain. I am giving you the service of the priesthood as a gift."

4. *Malachi 2:7* – "For the lips of a priest ought to preserve knowledge, because he is the messenger of the Lord Almighty and people seek instruction from his mouth."

5. *Hebrews 5:1* – "Every high priest is selected from among the people and is appointed to represent them in matters related to God, to offer gifts and sacrifices for sins."

Meaning: A *Kohen* (priest) was a sacred servant of God from the tribe of Levi, responsible for conducting Temple sacrifices, leading worship, and teaching the people. Aaron, the brother of Moses, was the first *Kohen Gadol* (High Priest). The role of the *Kohen* was to mediate between God and Israel, ensuring the nation's spiritual purity. Today, the priestly lineage is still recognized, with *Kohanim* having special roles in Jewish prayer and blessings.

Thirty-Three

LEVI

לֵוִי

Tribe of Levi, Priests of Israel

Verses:

1. *Genesis 29:34* – "Again she conceived, and when she gave birth to a son she said, 'Now at last my husband will become attached to me, because I have borne him three sons.' So he was named Levi."

2. *Exodus 32:26* – "Then Moses stood in the gate of the camp and said, 'Who is on the Lord's side? Come to me.' And all the sons of Levi gathered around him."

3. *Numbers 3:12* – "I have taken the Levites from among the Israelites in place of the first male offspring of every Israelite woman. The Levites are mine."

4. *Deuteronomy 10:8* – "At that time the Lord set apart the tribe of Levi to carry the Ark of the Covenant of the Lord, to stand before the Lord to minister and to pronounce blessings in his name."

5. *Malachi 2:4-5* – "And you shall know that I have sent this commandment unto you, that my covenant might be with Levi, says the Lord of hosts. My covenant was with him of life and peace."

Meaning: The tribe of *Levi* was set apart for priestly duties and temple service. Unlike the other tribes, the Levites were not given a land inheritance but were instead dedicated to God's service, relying on tithes and offerings. They served as teachers, priests, and caretakers of the Tabernacle and later the Temple. The Kohanim (priests) came specifically from the Levites, continuing their sacred duties until the Temple's destruction. Today, Levites still hold a special role in Jewish tradition, including blessing the congregation.

THIRTY-FOUR

ARK OF THE COVENANT

אֲרוֹן הַבְּרִית

THE SACRED CHEST HOLDING THE TABLETS OF THE LAW

Verses:

1. *Exodus 25:10* – "They shall make an ark of acacia wood, two cubits and a half shall be its length, a cubit and a half its breadth, and a cubit and a half its height."

2. *Exodus 25:21-22* – "Place the cover on top of the ark and put in the ark the tablets of the covenant law that I will give you. There, above the cover, between the two cherubim that are over the ark of the covenant law, I will meet with you and give you all my commands for the Israelites."

3. *Joshua 3:13* – "As soon as the priests who carry the ark of the Lord—the Lord of all the earth—set foot in the Jordan, its waters flowing downstream will be cut off and stand up in a heap."

4. *2 Samuel 6:2* – "And David arose and went with all the people who

were with him from Baale Judah to bring up from there the Ark of God, which is called by the Name, the name of the Lord Almighty, who is enthroned between the cherubim on the ark."

5. *Revelation 11:19* – "Then God's temple in heaven was opened, and within his temple was seen the Ark of his Covenant. And there came flashes of lightning, rumblings, peals of thunder, an earthquake and a severe hailstorm."

Meaning: The *Ark of the Covenant* was the most sacred object in Israelite worship, housing the stone tablets of the Ten Commandments, along with Aaron's rod and a jar of manna. It symbolized God's covenant with Israel and His presence among His people. The Ark was carried by Levites and was central to Israel's journey, from the wilderness to the conquest of Canaan. It was placed in the Holy of Holies in the Temple, accessible only by the High Priest once a year. Its final fate remains a mystery, contributing to its legendary status.

THIRTY-FIVE

KADOSH

קָדוֹשׁ

HOLY, SET APART

Verses:

1. *Leviticus 11:44* – "For I am the Lord your God. Consecrate yourselves therefore, and be holy, for I am holy."

2. *Isaiah 6:3* – "And one called to another and said: 'Holy, holy, holy is the Lord of hosts; the whole earth is full of His glory!'"

3. *Exodus 19:6* – "You shall be to me a kingdom of priests and a holy nation."

4. *Psalm 99:9* – "Exalt the Lord our God, and worship at His holy mountain; for the Lord our God is holy."

5. *1 Peter 1:15-16* – "But as He who called you is holy, you also be holy in all your conduct, since it is written, 'You shall be holy, for I am holy.'"

Meaning: *Kadosh* means "holy" or "set apart" and signifies something that is dedicated to God. In the Bible, God Himself is the ultimate source of holiness, and He calls His people to live in holiness. Holiness involves moral purity, spiritual devotion, and being distinct from the world. Objects, places, and people can be *kadosh* when they are sanctified for divine purposes. The concept is central to Jewish and Christian theology, emphasizing God's transcendence and the believer's call to righteousness.

Thirty-Six

TALLIT

טַלִּית

Prayer Shawl

Verses:

1. *Numbers 15:38-39* – "Speak to the Israelites and say to them: 'Throughout the generations to come you are to make tassels on the corners of your garments, with a blue cord on each tassel. You will have these tassels to look at and so you will remember all the commands of the Lord.'"

2. *Deuteronomy 22:12* – "You shall make yourself tassels on the four corners of the garment with which you cover yourself."

3. *Malachi 4:2* – "But for you who revere My name, the sun of righteousness will rise with healing in its wings."

4. *Matthew 9:20* – "And behold, a woman who had suffered from a discharge of blood for twelve years came up behind Him and touched the fringe of His garment."

5. *1 Samuel 24:5* – "Afterward, David's conscience was stricken for having cut off a corner of Saul's robe."

Meaning: The *Tallit* is a prayer shawl worn during morning prayers and special occasions. Its most significant feature is the *tzitzit* (fringes) on its corners, which serve as a reminder of God's commandments. The tallit is a symbol of faith and devotion, used in worship, study, and personal prayer. The tradition of wearing a tallit is deeply rooted in biblical commands and Jewish identity, representing spiritual protection and connection to divine teachings.

THIRTY-SEVEN

TEFILLIN

תְּפִלִּין

PHYLACTERIES, SMALL LEATHER BOXES WITH SCRIPTURES

Verses:

1. *Deuteronomy 6:8* – "You shall bind them as a sign on your hand, and they shall be as frontlets between your eyes."

2. *Exodus 13:9* – "It shall be as a sign to you on your hand and as a memorial between your eyes, that the Lord's law may be in your mouth."

3. *Deuteronomy 11:18* – "You shall therefore impress these words of mine on your heart and soul, and you shall bind them as a sign on your hand, and they shall be as frontlets between your eyes."

4. *Exodus 13:16* – "It shall be a sign on your hand and frontlets between your eyes, for by a strong hand the Lord brought us out of Egypt."

5. *Matthew 23:5* – "They do all their deeds to be seen by others, for they make their phylacteries broad and their fringes long."

Meaning: *Tefillin* are small black leather boxes containing Torah verses, bound with straps to the forehead and arm during weekday morning prayers. They serve as a physical reminder of God's commandments and the commitment to His laws. Worn close to the heart and mind, tefillin symbolize devotion to God in thought and action. This practice is deeply rooted in Jewish tradition and highlights obedience, faith, and spiritual discipline.

Thirty-Eight

MEZUZAH

מְזוּזָה

A Small Parchment with Torah Verses on Doorpost

Verses:

1. *Deuteronomy 6:9* – "You shall write them on the doorposts of your house and on your gates."
2. *Deuteronomy 11:20* – "Write them on the doorframes of your houses and on your gates."
3. *Exodus 12:7* – "Then they shall take some of the blood and put it on the two doorposts and the lintel of the houses in which they eat it."
4. *Proverbs 8:34* – "Blessed is the one who listens to me, watching daily at my doors, waiting at my doorway."
5. *Isaiah 57:8* – "Behind the door and the doorpost you have set up your memorial."

Meaning: The *Mezuzah* is a small case containing a handwritten parchment scroll with the *Shema* (Deuteronomy 6:4-9, 11:13-21). Affixed to the doorpost of Jewish homes, it serves as a constant reminder of God's presence and commandments. Touching the mezuzah upon entering or leaving a home is a gesture of faith and respect. It symbolizes divine protection and the sanctity of the home, reinforcing Jewish identity and commitment to God's laws.

Thirty-Nine

ECHAD

אֶחָד

One, Unity

Verses:

1. *Deuteronomy 6:4* – "Hear, O Israel: The Lord our God, the Lord is One."

2. *Zechariah 14:9* – "The Lord will be king over the whole earth. On that day there will be one Lord, and his name the only name."

3. *Isaiah 45:5* – "I am the Lord, and there is no other; apart from me there is no God."

4. *Mark 12:29* – "Jesus answered, 'The most important is, Hear, O Israel: The Lord our God, the Lord is one.'"

5. *Ephesians 4:5-6* – "One Lord, one faith, one baptism; one God and Father of all, who is over all and through all and in all."

Meaning: The word *Echad* means "one" and emphasizes the oneness and unity of God. This concept is foundational to Jewish monotheism, as expressed in the Shema prayer. It signifies that God is the singular, indivisible Creator and ruler of the universe. The idea of *Echad* also carries a deeper meaning of unity—not only of God but of His creation and people. It represents harmony and completeness in the divine order.

FORTY

GO'EL

גּוֹאֵל

REDEEMER

Verses:

1. *Job 19:25* – "For I know that my Redeemer lives, and at the last he will stand upon the earth."

2. *Isaiah 41:14* – "Do not fear, O Jacob, you worm, O little Israel, for I myself will help you, declares the Lord, your Redeemer, the Holy One of Israel."

3. *Isaiah 44:6* – "This is what the Lord says—Israel's King and Redeemer, the Lord Almighty: I am the first and I am the last; apart from me there is no God."

4. *Ruth 4:14* – "The women said to Naomi, 'Praise be to the Lord, who this day has not left you without a redeemer.'"

5. *Titus 2:14* – "Who gave Himself for us to redeem us from all wickedness and to purify for Himself a people that are His very own, eager to do what is good."

Meaning: *Go'el* ( )□□□□□□□means "redeemer" and refers to one who rescues, delivers, or buys back. In the Hebrew Bible, a *go'el* was a kinsman-redeemer, someone who had the responsibility to protect family members, restore land, or avenge wrongs. Spiritually, God is the ultimate *Go'el*, redeeming Israel from slavery, exile, and sin. The concept of redemption extends to messianic beliefs, where the Redeemer brings ultimate salvation and restoration.

Forty-One

YOM KIPPUR

יוֹם כִּפּוּר

Day of Atonement

Verses:

1. *Leviticus 16:30* – "For on this day shall atonement be made for you to cleanse you. You shall be clean before the Lord from all your sins."

2. *Leviticus 23:27* – "The tenth day of this seventh month is the Day of Atonement. Hold a sacred assembly and deny yourselves, and present a food offering to the Lord."

3. *Numbers 29:7* – "On the tenth day of this seventh month you shall have a holy convocation and shall afflict yourselves; you shall not do any work."

4. *Isaiah 1:18* – "Come now, let us settle the matter, says the Lord. Though your sins are like scarlet, they shall be as white as snow; though they are red like crimson, they shall become like wool."

5. *Hebrews 9:12* – "He did not enter by means of the blood of goats and calves; but He entered the Most Holy Place once for all by His own blood, thus obtaining eternal redemption."

Meaning: Yom Kippur, the Day of Atonement, is the holiest day in the Jewish calendar. It is a solemn day of fasting, prayer, and repentance, where individuals seek forgiveness from God and others. The biblical rituals included the High Priest entering the Holy of Holies and the scapegoat ceremony. Today, it is observed through confession, prayer (*vidui*), and seeking reconciliation. Yom Kippur emphasizes divine mercy, spiritual cleansing, and renewal of one's relationship with God.

Forty-Two

ROSH HASHANAH

רֹאשׁ הַשָּׁנָה

Jewish New Year

Verses:

1. *Leviticus 23:24* – "Speak to the people of Israel, saying, 'In the seventh month, on the first day of the month, you shall observe a day of solemn rest, a memorial proclaimed with a blast of trumpets, a holy convocation.'"

2. *Numbers 29:1* – "On the first day of the seventh month you shall have a holy convocation. You shall not do any ordinary work. It is a day for you to blow the trumpets."

3. *Psalm 81:3* – "Blow the trumpet at the new moon, at the full moon, on our feast day."

4. *Nehemiah 8:10* – "Go your way, eat the fat, and drink sweet wine and send portions to anyone who has nothing ready, for this day is holy to our Lord. And do not be grieved, for the joy of the Lord is your strength."

5. *Revelation 11:15* – "Then the seventh angel blew his trumpet, and there were loud voices in heaven, saying, 'The kingdom of the world has become the kingdom of our Lord and of His Christ, and He shall reign forever and ever.'"

Meaning: Rosh Hashanah, the Jewish New Year, marks the beginning of the High Holy Days and a period of introspection and renewal. It is known as the "Day of Judgment" (*Yom HaDin*) and the "Day of Remembrance" (*Yom Hazikaron*), when God evaluates human actions. The central practice is the blowing of the *shofar* (ram's horn), symbolizing divine awakening and repentance. It is a time of reflection, prayer, and seeking blessings for the coming year. Rosh Hashanah emphasizes new beginnings and spiritual growth.

FORTY-THREE

SUKKOT

סֻכּוֹת

FEAST OF TABERNACLES

Verses:

1. *Leviticus 23:42-43* – "You shall dwell in booths for seven days. All native Israelites shall dwell in booths, that your generations may know that I made the children of Israel dwell in booths when I brought them out of the land of Egypt."

2. *Deuteronomy 16:13* – "You shall keep the Feast of Booths seven days, when you have gathered in the produce from your threshing floor and your winepress."

3. *Zechariah 14:16* – "Then the survivors from all the nations that have attacked Jerusalem will go up year after year to worship the King, the Lord Almighty, and to celebrate the Feast of Tabernacles."

4. *John 7:37-38* – "On the last and greatest day of the festival, Jesus stood and said in a loud voice, 'Let anyone who is thirsty come to me and drink. Whoever believes in me, as Scripture has said, rivers of living water will flow from within them.'"

5. *Nehemiah 8:17* – "And all the assembly of those who had returned from the captivity made booths and lived in the booths, for from the

days of Joshua the son of Nun to that day the people of Israel had not done so. And there was very great rejoicing."

Meaning: Sukkot, or the Feast of Tabernacles, is a biblical festival celebrating God's provision and protection during Israel's 40 years in the wilderness. It is observed by building temporary booths (*sukkot*) to recall the shelters used in the desert. Sukkot is also a time of joy and gratitude for the harvest. Prophetically, it represents the future messianic age when all nations will worship God in unity.

FORTY-FOUR

OLAM HABA

עוֹלָם הַבָּא

THE WORLD TO COME, AFTERLIFE

Verses:

1. *Daniel 12:2* – "Many of those who sleep in the dust of the earth shall awake, some to everlasting life, and some to shame and everlasting contempt."

2. *Isaiah 65:17* – "For behold, I create new heavens and a new earth, and the former things shall not be remembered or come into mind."

3. *Psalm 16:11* – "You make known to me the path of life; in your presence, there is fullness of joy; at your right hand are pleasures forevermore."

4. *Mishnah, Sanhedrin 10:1* – "All Israel has a share in the world to come, as it is said: 'Your people are all righteous; they shall inherit the land forever.'"

5. *Matthew 19:29* – "And everyone who has left houses or brothers or sisters or father or mother or children or lands, for my name's sake, will receive a hundredfold and will inherit eternal life."

Meaning: Olam HaBa, meaning "the world to come," refers to the future state of existence after this life. It is a foundational concept in Jewish thought, describing the eternal reward for the righteous and the renewal of the world in divine perfection. While interpretations differ—some see it as a spiritual afterlife, others as a messianic age on earth—it represents hope, justice, and ultimate closeness to God.

FORTY-FIVE

GAN EDEN

גַּן עֵדֶן

GARDEN OF EDEN

Verses:

1. *Genesis 2:8* – "And the Lord God planted a garden in Eden, in the east, and there He put the man whom He had formed."

2. *Genesis 3:24* – "He drove out the man, and at the east of the Garden of Eden He placed the cherubim and a flaming sword that turned every way to guard the way to the tree of life."

3. *Ezekiel 28:13* – "You were in Eden, the garden of God; every precious stone adorned you."

4. *Joel 2:3* – "Before them the land is like the Garden of Eden, behind them, a desolate wilderness—nothing escapes them."

5. *Revelation 2:7* – "To the one who overcomes, I will grant to eat of the tree of life, which is in the paradise of God."

Meaning: Gan Eden, or the Garden of Eden, represents a paradise where humanity was created and initially lived in perfect harmony with God. It symbolizes purity, innocence, and divine blessing. After Adam and Eve's disobedience, they were expelled, marking the loss of an ideal world. In Jewish and Christian traditions, Gan Eden is also seen as a future place of spiritual reward for the righteous, signifying restoration and eternal peace.

Forty-Six

SHEKINAH

שְׁכִינָה

God's Divine Presence

Verses:

1. *Exodus 40:34* – "Then the cloud covered the Tent of Meeting, and the glory of the Lord filled the tabernacle."
2. *1 Kings 8:11* – "And the priests could not stand to minister because of the cloud, for the glory of the Lord filled the house of the Lord."
3. *Psalm 91:1* – "Whoever dwells in the shelter of the Most High will rest in the shadow of the Almighty."
4. *Isaiah 6:3* – "Holy, holy, holy is the Lord Almighty; the whole earth is full of His glory."
5. *Revelation 21:3* – "And I heard a loud voice from the throne saying, 'Behold, the dwelling place of God is with man.'"

Meaning: Shekinah refers to the manifestation of God's divine presence. Though the term itself does not appear in the Bible, it is used in Jewish thought to describe God's nearness, particularly in the tabernacle, temple, and moments of revelation. Shekinah represents God's guidance, comfort, and presence among His people. It is also linked to the future restoration when God will dwell fully among humanity.

FORTY-SEVEN

NAVI

נָבִיא

PROPHET

Verses:

1. *Deuteronomy 18:18* – "I will raise up for them a prophet like you from among their brothers. I will put my words in his mouth, and he will tell them everything I command him."

2. *Jeremiah 1:5* – "Before I formed you in the womb I knew you, before you were born I set you apart; I appointed you as a prophet to the nations."

3. *Amos 3:7* – "Surely the Sovereign Lord does nothing without revealing his plan to his servants the prophets."

4. *Hosea 12:10* – "I spoke to the prophets, gave them many visions, and told parables through them."

5. *2 Chronicles 20:20* – "Believe in the Lord your God, and you will be established; believe his prophets, and you will succeed."

Meaning: The Hebrew word *Navi* refers to a prophet, one who serves as a divine messenger, speaking on behalf of God. Prophets were chosen to guide, warn, and reveal God's will to the people. The role of a *Navi* was not self-appointed; it required divine calling, as seen in Moses, Jeremiah, and Isaiah. They often faced resistance but remained steadfast in delivering their message.

FORTY-EIGHT

SEFER

סֵפֶר

SCROLL OR BOOK

Verses:

1. *Deuteronomy 17:18* – "When he takes the throne of his kingdom, he is to write for himself on a scroll a copy of this law."

2. *Joshua 1:8* – "This Book of the Law shall not depart from your mouth, but you shall meditate on it day and night."

3. *Psalm 40:7* – "Then I said, 'Here I am, I have come—it is written about me in the scroll.'"

4. *Jeremiah 36:2* – "Take a scroll and write on it all the words I have spoken to you concerning Israel, Judah, and all the nations."

5. *Revelation 5:1* – "Then I saw in the right hand of him who sat on the throne a scroll with writing on both sides and sealed with seven seals."

Meaning: The word *Sefer* means scroll or book, often referring to scripture or sacred writings. In ancient times, religious teachings, laws, and prophecies were recorded on scrolls to preserve divine instruction. The Torah, prophetic writings, and wisdom literature were all written as *sefarim* (plural of *sefer*), signifying their enduring authority.